VOLCANOES

by Sandra Markle

Illustrations by Jo-Ellen C. Bosson

SCHOLASTIC INC.

New York   Toronto   London   Auckland   Sydney
Mexico City   New Delhi   Hong Kong   Buenos Aires

With love, for Brad and Katrina Jeffery

CAN YOU BELIEVE . . .

NOTE TO PARENTS AND TEACHERS: This book is intended to help children develop skills and concepts related to the following processes: that volcanoes are part of how Earth's inner heat changes the surface crust—both slowly and suddenly; that volcanoes have a natural life cycle through which they are born, grow, and die. Children will also see how technology is being used to monitor volcanoes in the hope of warning people in time to escape an eruption. "The surface of the earth changes. Some changes are due to slow processes, such as erosion and weathering, and some changes are due to rapid processes, such as landslides, volcanic eruptions, and earthquakes." (National Science Education Standards as identified by the National Academy of Sciences for K-4 students.)

Can you believe

what happened to this city started deep inside the earth?

These houses in Iceland were buried in **ash** from an erupting **volcano**. But what made the volcano erupt? And why did the volcano form at that spot instead of somewhere else on Earth? Now you can answer all your burning volcano questions. You'll find out why some volcanoes cause deadly mud slides, clouds of burning gas, and lightning. Along the way, you'll discover lots of amazing facts about volcanoes—some may even seem unbelievable!

Like people, volcanoes have a life cycle. They are born, grow, and finally die.

So what powers up the volcanic process?

A. heat
B. waves
C. wind

Turn the page and start exploring to find out!

Can you believe

volcanoes start because of heat deep in the earth?

TRY IT YOURSELF!

See for yourself what happens to start the process that leads to a volcanic eruption. Be sure to ask permission to do this activity and have an adult help you use the stove.

1. Put a plain chocolate candy bar into a pan.

2. Heat on low heat, watching what happens. As the candy warms up, the solid chocolate becomes a thick, soft paste.

The interior of the earth is much hotter than the stove—hot enough to melt rock, forming a plasticlike material called **magma**.

DID YOU KNOW?

The biggest volcano in the world is Mauna Loa on the island of Hawaii.

Compared to the rest of its mass, Earth's crust is as thin as an eggshell. Like a dropped egg, Earth's crust is cracked into pieces. Each piece is called a **plate**.

Can you believe

these plates are moving?

This map shows Earth's plates and the arrows show the direction each plate is moving.

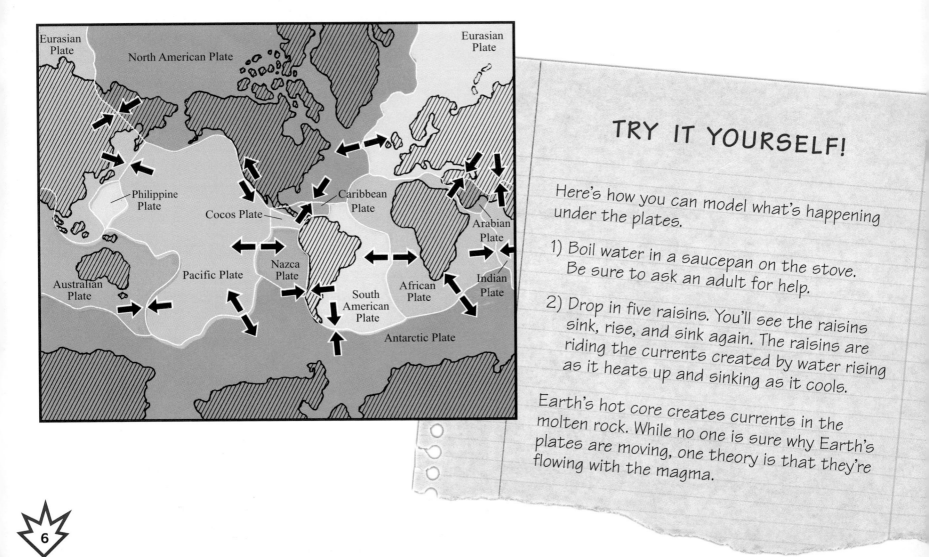

TRY IT YOURSELF!

Here's how you can model what's happening under the plates.

1) Boil water in a saucepan on the stove. Be sure to ask an adult for help.

2) Drop in five raisins. You'll see the raisins sink, rise, and sink again. The raisins are riding the currents created by water rising as it heats up and sinking as it cools.

Earth's hot core creates currents in the molten rock. While no one is sure why Earth's plates are moving, one theory is that they're flowing with the magma.

These bubbles are gases seeping out of a **vent**, or opening, in the seabed. The gases are escaping from hot magma. If the crack opens wider, magma will reach the surface and flow out. When it is on the surface, magma is called **lava**. Wherever Earth's plates are moving apart, lava fills the gap forming new land. Look at the map of Earth's plates and you'll see this type of spreading is happening deep down on the floor of the Atlantic Ocean. But this is a slow, gentle process.

So where do violent volcanic eruptions usually happen?

A. where Earth's plates bump together

B. where the sun heats up rock

C. where rivers empty into oceans

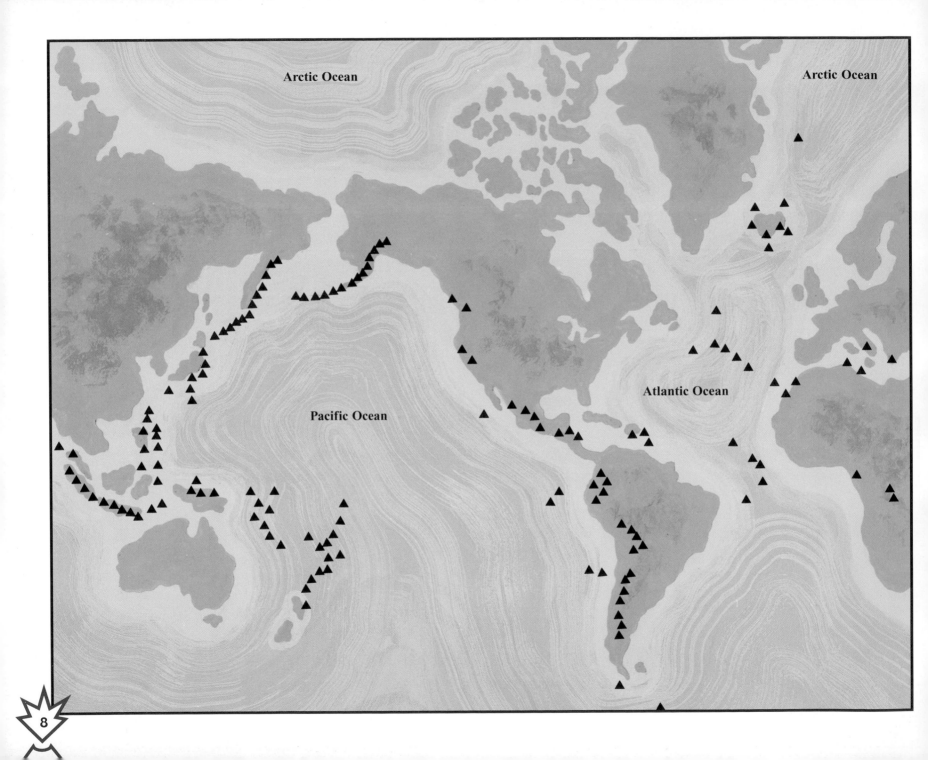

Arctic Ocean

Arctic Ocean

Pacific Ocean

Atlantic Ocean

Can you believe

most volcanoes form where Earth's plates bump together?

Look at this map to see where the world's volcanoes are located. No wonder the Pacific Ocean is said to have a ring of fire!

Volcanologists, people who study volcanoes, believe that as the plates rub against each other, they generate heat.

What do you think happens next?

A. Magma rises through cracks.
B. Globs of magma shoot into the air.
C. Magma flows out over the ground.

Can you believe

Besides being broken into plates, Earth's crust has lots of small cracks. Here lava is squirting out of a crack.

crater

magma chamber

A volcano is a mountain that forms as lava erupts out of one spot, a vent, and piles up, layer upon layer, over time. The volcano develops its own plumbing. Here you can see that a magma chamber stores molten rock until it rises to the surface through a pipe. There, the lava often pools in a more or less circular basin, a **crater**, surrounded by a rim of cooled lava.

Volcanoes that continue to erupt are called active volcanoes. Volcanoes that contain molten rock but haven't erupted for a long period of time are dormant—inactive but could become active again at any time. Volcanoes that no longer contain molten rock are extinct—they will never erupt again.

Can you believe

some people have witnessed the birth of a volcano?

In 1943, Dominic Pulido, a farmer in central Mexico, was out working in his cornfield when he heard a deep rumble like thunder underground. The trees around him shook as he watched a little mound of dirt swell up and puff gray volcanic ash. There was a strong rotten-egg smell. Then with a loud hiss, the mound cracked open. This was the start of the Paricutín volcano.

Soon lava was shooting out of Paricutín. What had been a little mound grew into a mountain. In its first year, the cone-shaped mountain grew to 1,100 feet (336 meters). Volcanologists were delighted to have a chance to watch this volcano grow. As Paricutín continued to grow over the next eight years, it only added another 290 feet (88 meters) to its height, but it buried two whole villages. Ash covered the surrounding forests, too, destroying most of the trees.

The ash and lava spewed by an active volcano can cause a lot of damage. But there is another danger associated with volcanic eruptions.

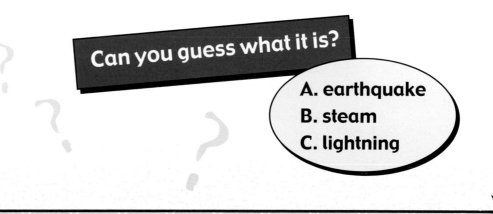

Can you guess what it is?

A. earthquake
B. steam
C. lightning

Can you believe

lightning can strike
during volcanic
eruptions?

TRY IT YOURSELF!

1) Blow up a balloon.

2) Rub it against your hair.

All matter is made up of tiny building blocks called atoms. Rubbing your hair knocks loose some charged bits from the atoms, called **electrons**. As the electrons jump from your head to the balloon, you'll hear crackles from the flowing electrical charge.

The collision of lots of bits of ash spewed out by a volcano knocks loose electrons, creating a much more powerful charge—a **lightning** bolt.

Can you believe
volcanic ash can block out the sun?

Look at all the steam and ash erupting from Mount Usu in Japan!
What do you think will happen to the city of Touya?

There's so much ash from Mount Pinatubo in the Philippines that it blocks the noonday sun. If you've ever opened a can of soda that shot out foam, you've discovered the process that made all this volcanic ash. Magma contains water vapor (water in the form of a gas) and other gases. As the magma rises toward the surface, these gases form bubbles. If the magma is thick, the gas can't escape—it's trapped inside the magma, like the bubbles in an unopened can of soda. When the magma reaches the surface, the trapped bubbles make it explode upward, just like when you open a can of warm soda. The force of the explosion blows the magma to bits, forming volcanic ash. No wonder the people in this picture have masks over their faces!

This is a plaster cast made of a man who died while trying to escape when hot gas and ash erupted from Mount Vesuvius in Italy almost two thousand years ago. This man was one of many victims when Mount Vesuvius erupted, destroying the ancient Roman city of Pompeii. A cloud of hot gas and ash struck so suddenly that people died before they could flee. Then the city was buried under ash, which preserved everything. More than a thousand years later, researchers dug out the city. They found the remains of buildings, gardens, food, people, and even a pet dog. This gave researchers a unique view of life in ancient Rome.

In 1980, whole forests of trees were knocked down when Mount Saint Helens in Washington State erupted. This time, rock, ash, and gas were blasted out at nearly supersonic speed. The blast that did all this damage lasted only about ninety seconds. Luckily, people had been warned this volcano was likely to erupt, so few people were in the area. Still, fifty-seven people were killed.

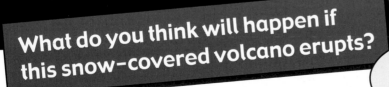

What do you think will happen if this snow-covered volcano erupts?

A. The lava will harden instantly.
B. The ice will melt.
C. The ice will turn to steam.

20

Can you believe

the melting ice will create a thick mud flow?

Mix water with dirt and you get mud. When that mud is pouring down the side of a steep volcano, it forms a raging river of mud and rocks, called a **lahar**. Here you can see a woman and her daughter caught in a lahar that rolled off the slopes of Mount Pinatubo. In 1985, when the Nevado del Ruiz volcano erupted in Colombia, a lahar swept through villages, destroying everything in its path. The town of Armero was hit the hardest. Three-fourths of its 28,700 residents were killed—that's more than 20,000 people.

Volcanoes can cause serious damage to cities and even kill people. Volcanoes also cause changes to Earth's surface.

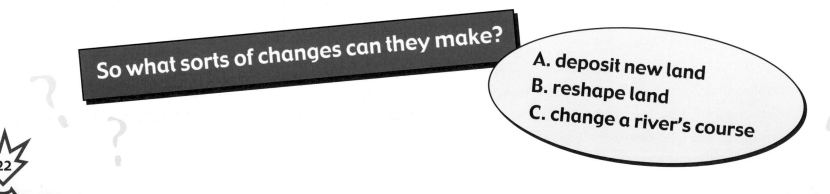

So what sorts of changes can they make?

A. deposit new land
B. reshape land
C. change a river's course

Can you believe

volcanoes change Earth in all those ways?

Here you can see one of Earth's youngest islands—Surtsey. The process that created it started on November 8, 1963, off the mainland of Iceland, when lava poured out onto the seafloor. The cold water took away a lot of the heat energy from the lava, making it cool and harden. Lava continued to pour out, building up layer upon layer. In just a week, the lava formed a volcano more than 400 feet (130 meters) tall—high enough for the top to be above water. The new island was born! The volcano kept on growing for three more years, making the island bigger. After it stopped erupting, however, ocean waves washed away some of the land, making Surtsey smaller.

DID YOU KNOW?

Mauna Loa volcano in Hawaii is actually taller than Mount Everest, which is listed as Earth's highest mountain. Mauna Loa just looks shorter because only its peak is above water.

This glowing red liquid is molten lava. The black lump is a lava bomb, a glob of hot lava tossed into the air. When volcanoes explosively eject lava bombs, the material starts to harden on its way back down to the ground. That gives the lava bomb its teardrop shape. The volcano that tossed out this lava bomb is active all the time and ejects fresh rock material several times a day. Those lava bombs always land on ice.

Where in the world is this ice-covered volcano?

A. Greenland
B. Alaska
C. Antarctica

Can you believe

Mount Erebus is in Antarctica?

It may seem hard to believe that a land covered by ice year-round could have active volcanoes, but it does. Mount Erebus is one of the best known because its lava lake is continually active. It's this bubbling lake that tosses out lava bombs. Mt. Erebus is unusual in more ways than one. Besides erupting in a frozen world, it is in the middle of one of Earth's plates. While most volcanoes form where two pieces of the crust collide, some form at hot spots— places where hot magma melts through the crust.

Sometimes volcanoes change Earth's shape very quickly. That's what happened on September 23, 1995, when Mount Ruapehu in New Zealand suddenly erupted. A series of three big explosions launched the water from its crater lake, chunks of rock from the mountaintop, and ash and molten lava from its vent. This instantly changed the mountain's shape. The eruption also started a lahar that sent mud and debris rushing down the mountainside. The lahar poured into streams, changing the drainage pattern of the Whangaehu River.

DID YOU KNOW?

When a volcanic eruption ends, the top of the volcano may collapse into its empty magma chamber. If this big basin fills with rainwater and melted snow, it becomes a lake.

How do volcanologists predict when a volcano like Ruapehu is likely to erupt?

A. check the local weather conditions
B. monitor the mountain's shape
C. watch plants growing on the mountain

Can you believe

volcanoes may swell up before they erupt?

The key to judging when a volcano is likely to erupt is finding out how close the magma is getting to the mountaintop. One way to tell where the magma is inside a volcano is to check if the mountain is swelling. Of course, the volcano doesn't swell enough for people to see it getting larger. So volcanologists use special instruments to help them tell when and where the volcano is swelling. **Tiltmeters** measure even the tiniest tilting of the volcano's slopes. Special lasers measure the exact distance between two points on the mountain, showing any expansion of the volcano. Global Positioning System (GPS) receivers bounce radio signals off a network of twenty-four Earth-orbiting satellites. They pinpoint the exact position of certain spots on the volcano's side—another way to monitor and record movement.

Volcanologists also monitor any tremors or earthquakes inside the volcano, using an instrument called a **seismograph**. Here you can see the one being used to monitor Mount Erebus in Antarctica. This tool has a solid base anchored into the ground, which allows it to move during a tremor. The base is attached to a recording device—often a computer. When there is no movement inside the volcano, the seismograph records a steady pen line on paper. Anytime there is a tremor, the seismograph records a spiked line—the bigger the spike the more violent the tremor. Volcanologist Steve Mattox said, "If I could only have one tool to monitor a volcano, it would be a seismographic station. Tremors show magma movement inside the volcano."

Can you believe

some gases may provide clues that a volcano is likely to erupt?

Here you can see volcanologists collecting samples of the gas escaping from the hot lava. They're checking for the presence of a chemical like sulfur. From studies of past eruptions, volcanologists have learned that an increase in certain gases can be a sign that magma is rising inside the volcano.

Once they collect all these clues about a volcano, how well can volcanologists predict when a volcano will erupt?

In 1980, volcanologists did a great job of predicting the eruption of Mount Saint Helens in time for most people to move to safety. Again, in 1991, volcanologists warned that Mount Pinatubo was likely to erupt even though it had been quiet for about 600 years. More than 10,000 people fled in time to escape the violent eruption that followed.

See all the chunks of rock erupting
out of Mount Galeras? Predicting eruptions helps
people, but monitoring volcanoes can be a dangerous job.
In 1993, Andrew MacFarlane was one of a group monitoring
Mount Galeras in Colombia when it suddenly erupted. He reported:
"We heard a little pop. So we quickly started downhill. Then boom!
We turned and saw a huge cloud starting to roll toward us. We ran for
it, but glowing chunks of rock slammed into the hillside around us.
Some landed on other rocks. Then these shattered, shooting out
sharp chunks."

While no gear can protect volcanologists from a violent eruption, there are special suits to protect researchers from being burned. Here you can see volcanologists collecting lava samples in suits made of a fire-resistant cloth. One of them, Christina Heliker, said, "If a glob of lava drops on the cloth, it chars but doesn't burn or melt on our skin." These volcanologists are also wearing the same kinds of hoods and insulated leather gloves firefighters sometimes wear. Heliker reported that the hand protection still isn't enough. "Tools that have been dipped into the lava are glowing red when we pull them out. The cables and hammers are so hot that we have to use extra gloves like potholders to handle them. Even then, we can only hold them for a few seconds!"

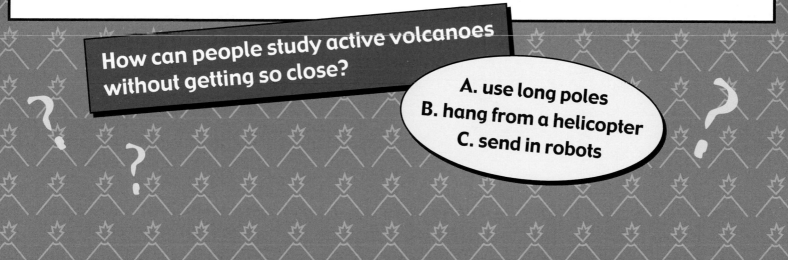

How can people study active volcanoes without getting so close?

A. use long poles
B. hang from a helicopter
C. send in robots

Can you believe

robots can help people study volcanoes safely?

Here a robot called Dante II is getting a lift to the top of Mount Spurr, an active volcano about 80 miles (128 kilometers) from Anchorage, Alaska. Volcanologists wanted to understand this volcano better because its eruptions were a threat to Anchorage and to planes flying overhead. Because it was very dangerous to send scientists into the active crater at Mount Spurr, Carnegie Mellon University's Robotics Institute designed Dante II to do the job. Dante II's visit to Mount Spurr was also a test of this robot's abilities to operate in difficult volcanic terrain similar to what it might encounter on Mars.

Safe in Anchorage, William "Red" Whittaker "drove" the robot using radio controls. Whittaker wore special glasses that let him see what Dante II was viewing with its video camera eyes that could look all the way around itself. Red could guide the robot to move one foot at a time or four feet at once. Or he could instruct the robot to move ahead on its own. Then Dante II's computer evaluated input from its cameras and a laser mapping system. This let the robot move around rocks and cross the uneven terrain without tipping over. As soon as Dante II reached a **fumarole**—a hole where steam and gases escape—its sensors reported what chemicals were in the gas and how hot it was. In the future, robots like Dante II may stand in for people studying other dangerous places. Imagine being safe on Earth, guiding a robot that's exploring Mars!

Can you believe

this plant is growing on old lava?

After lava pours out of a volcano, it quickly cools and hardens. Then wind and water begin to break down the rock. Volcanic ash may break down quickly, but it takes a very long time for the surface of rock like this to break down into rock grains. Finally, seeds of plants that land in cracks or among the loose rock grains sprout and take root.

DID YOU KNOW?

Plants were the first living things to settle on the island of Surtsey. The seeds of hardy sea sandworts washed ashore and sprouted. Later, seabirds started nesting there, hatching Surtsey's first babies.

Can you believe
some people like to live near volcanoes?

Volcanic rocks contain a lot of minerals that plants need to grow. So even though volcanic eruptions are often violent, people are willing to live near these mountains when they're quiet.

DID YOU KNOW?

Sometimes people decide to stay and fight rather than run away from an erupting volcano. In 1973, the people of Heimaey, Iceland, sprayed lava with seawater to stop it from reaching homes and the harbor.

Besides producing fertile soil, volcanic activity helps people in other ways. This picture provides a clue to what volcanoes do.

What do you think Earth's heat energy did for this city?

A. produced the electricity
B. burned the garbage
C. fueled the cars

Can you believe

volcanic activity can produce electricity?

The process of generating electricity starts when magma heats up water in the ground. This is known as **geothermal** water. Next, people drill a well to tap this hot water. Sometimes, releasing the trapped water causes it to turn to steam. Like wind blowing a pinwheel, the steam spins giant blades on machines called turbines. That produces electricity. With other methods, the hot groundwater is used to heat up another liquid that boils at a lower temperature than water. This liquid then turns to steam, powering up the turbines that generate electricity.

In Iceland and other parts of the world, geothermal water is also used to warm greenhouses. There vegetables and flowers can be grown year-round.

Can you believe

people bathe in geothermal water for their health?

Many people believe soaking in geothermal water helps heal inflamed joints and muscles. Besides feeling good, geothermal water is often rich in dissolved **minerals**, the building blocks of rocks. The ancient Romans even used geothermal water as medicine to treat eye and skin diseases. Whether it's a real cure or not, people have always enjoyed relaxing in Earth's natural hot springs.

Here you can see volcanologist Andrew MacFarlane taking a close look at rocks. He said, "Extinct volcanoes are a good place to mine minerals, like silver, nickel, copper, and gold. When the volcano was active, magma heated up water in the ground and that dissolved minerals out of deep rocks. Then this water flowed into spaces in other rocks. Once the water cooled, it deposited its mineral load. Studying active volcanoes teaches me what minerals I'm likely to find around extinct volcanoes. It also lets me learn how deep those mineral deposits are likely to be."

Can you believe

volcanoes are part of Earth's natural processes?

Magma reaches surface

Active volcano

Remains of dead volcano

44

Now you know how heat energy deep inside Earth powers up a volcano. The process that caused the volcano to be born, grow, and die is just part of what naturally happens to change Earth's surface. Sometimes, when lava simply flows out, the changes happen slowly. Other times, when there's a violent volcanic eruption, Earth's surface changes suddenly. Then volcanoes are part of Earth's natural processes gone wild!

Glossary/Index/Pronunciation Guide

ash Bits of glassy dust that erupt from a volcano in a cloud before settling to the ground. 3, 13, 15-19

crater [KRAY tur] The nearly circle-shaped basin at the top of a volcano. 11

electron [ee LEK tron] One of the parts of an atom, the basic building block of all matter. 15

fumarole [FYOO muh rohl] Hole in the side of a volcano where steam and gases escape. 37

geothermal [gee oh THER muhl] Term used to describe something heated by Earth's natural heat energy. 41-42

lahar [LAH hahr] A flow of mud and debris caused by a volcanic eruption. 21, 26

lava [LAH vuh] Molten rock flowing out of a volcano. 7, 10-13, 23-26, 35, 38, 45

lava bomb Glob of molten material explosively tossed out of a volcano during an eruption. 24-25

lightning A powerful electrical charge that appears as a flash of light in the sky. 14-15

magma [MAG muh] Molten rock within Earth. 4, 6-7, 9, 17, 25, 27-30

mineral [MIH nuh ruhl] Nonliving solid, like gold and silver, that occurs naturally in rocks and in the ground. 42-43

plate Section of Earth's crust. 5-7, 9-10

seismograph [SIZE muh graf] An instrument for recording volcanic tremors. 29

tiltmeter [TILT mee tuhr] An instrument for measuring ground tilt. 28

vent An opening in Earth's crust through which volcanic material escapes. 7, 11

volcano [vahl KAY noh] A mountain created by the buildup of volcanic material. 3-4, 9-45

volcanologist [VAHL kuh *nahl* uh jist] Someone who studies volcanoes. 9, 13, 27-35

PHOTO CREDITS:
Cover: Danilo Donadoni/Bruce Coleman
p. 2: W. Ferchland/Bruce Coleman
p. 5: Skip Jeffery
p. 7: Carl Roessler/Earth Scenes
p. 10: Tui De Roy
p. 12: R.E. Wilcox/USGS
p. 14: E.R. Degginger/Earth Scenes
p. 16: Itsuo Inouye/AP Photo
p. 17: Itsuo Inouye/AP Photo
p. 18: Werner Keller
p. 19: Annie Griffith/Bruce Coleman
p. 20: Tony Hughes
p. 21: Pat Rogue/AP Photo
p. 22: Brad Lewis
p. 23: Norman Tomalin/Bruce Coleman
p. 24 (2): Phillip Kyle
p. 25: Skip Jeffery
p. 27: Tui De Roy
p. 28: S. Honnorex/Bruce Coleman
p. 29: Skip Jeffery; inset Breck Kent/Earth Scenes
p. 30: C. Heliker/USGS
p. 31: Tony Hughes
p. 32: Stanley Williams
p. 34: J.D. Griggs/USGS
p. 36: The Robotics Institute, Carnegie Mellon University
p. 37: The Robotics Institute, Carnegie Mellon University
p. 38: Skip Jeffery
p. 39: Skip Jeffery
p. 40: Skip Jeffery
p. 41: Skip Jeffery
p. 42: Skip Jeffery
p. 43: Andrew MacFarlane
p. 44: Magma reaches surface, E.R. Digginger/Bruce
Coleman; Active volcano, Masha Nordbye/Bruce Coleman;
Remains of dead volcano, P. Deggingee/Bruce Coleman

Acknowledgments: The author would like to thank the following persons for sharing their expertise and enthusiasm: John Bares, Carnegie Mellon Robotics Institute; Christina Heliker and Don Swanson, the U.S. Geological Survey; Phillip Kyle, New Mexico Institute of Mining and Technology; Andrew MacFarlane; Steve Mattox, Assistant Professor of Geology, Grand Valley State University, Michigan; and William "Red" Whittaker. As always, a special thanks to Skip Jeffery for his help and support.

ISBN 0-439-35611-3

Text copyright © 2002 by Sandra Markle.
Illustrations copyright © 2002 by Scholastic Inc.

All rights reserved.
Published by Scholastic Inc., 557 Broadway, New York, NY 10012.
SCHOLASTIC and associated logos are trademarks
and/or registered trademarks of Scholastic Inc.

12 11 10 9 8 7 6 5 4 3 2   6 7 8/0

Printed in the U.S.A.   40
First Scholastic printing, February 2002